How Things Grow

From Acorn to Oak Tree

By Jan Kottke

Welcome
Books

Children's Press
A Division of Grolier Publishing
New York / London / Hong Kong / Sydney
Danbury, Connecticut

Photo Credits: Cover and all photos by Dwight Kuhn
Contributing Editor: Mark Beyer
Book Design: MaryJane Wojciechowski

Visit Children's Press on the Internet at:
http://publishing.grolier.com

Cataloging-in-Publication Data

Kottke, Jan
 From acorn to oak tree / by Jan Kottke.
    p.   cm.—(How things grow)
    Includes bibliographical references and index.
    Summary: This book describes how acorns become oak trees.
    ISBN 0-516-23306-8 (lib. bdg.)— 0-516-23506-0 (pbk.)
    1.   Oak—Life cycles—Juvenile literature
[1.   Oak   2.   Trees]   I.   Title   II.   Series
    2000
583'.46—dc21

99-058216

Contents

Acorns grow on oak tree branches.

Acorns are the seeds of an oak tree.

5

Acorns drop to the ground.

In the spring, the acorn cracks open.

A tiny **shoot** pushes out of its hard shell.

7

The shoot pushes itself into the ground.

A small **sprout** pushes up from the acorn.

9

The shoot becomes the **root** of the oak tree.

The sprout unfolds into tiny **leaves.**

11

The oak tree begins to grow.

It is small and has few leaves.

13

Many years pass before the tree grows tall.

The acorn is now an oak tree.

15

Each spring the oak tree sprouts leaves.

These leaves grow on branches.

17

Tiny flowers grow next to the sprouting leaves.

The flowers help the tree to make acorns.

19

Acorns grow fat during spring and summer.

Soon they will fall off the tree.

21

New Words

acorns (**ay**-korns) seeds of an oak tree

leaves (**leevz**) the flat, thin, green parts
of trees

root (**root**) the part of a tree that grows
under the ground

shoot (**shoot**) the part of a plant that
grows from the seed into the ground

sprout (**sprowt**) the part of a plant that
grows from the seed out of the ground

To Find Out More

Books

Acorn Magic
by Maggie Stern and Donna Ruff
Greenwillow Books

The Gift of the Tree
by Alvin Tresselt and Henri Sorensen
Lothrop Lee & Shepard Books

Up the Tall Tree
by Rosie Hankin and Kareen Taylerson
Raintree Steck-Vaughn Publishers

Web Site

A to Z of Trees
http://edu.leeds.ac.uk/~edu/technology/epb97/forest/aztrees.htm
At this site you can learn about many kinds of trees. There are a lot of pictures for you to look at.

Index

About the Author

Jan Kottke is the owner/director of several preschools in the Tidewater area of Virginia. A lifelong early education professional, she is completing a phonics reading series for preschoolers.

Reading Consultants

Kris Flynn, Coordinator, Small School District Literacy, The San Diego County Office of Education

Shelly Forys, Certified Reading Recovery Specialist, W.J. Sahnow Elementary School, Waterloo, IL

Peggy McNamara, Professor, Bank Street College of Education, Reading and Literacy Program